P9-AQD-927

Dropping In On...
Orlando

Melanie Waxler

Educational Media

rourkeeducationalmedia.com

Scan for Related Titles
and Teacher Resources

Before Reading:

Building Academic Vocabulary and Background Knowledge

Before reading a book, it is important to tap into what your child or students already know about the topic. This will help them develop their vocabulary, increase their reading comprehension, and make connections across the curriculum.

1. Look at the cover of the book. What will this book be about?
2. What do you already know about the topic?
3. Let's study the Table of Contents. What will you learn about in the book's chapters?
4. What would you like to learn about this topic? Do you think you might learn about it from this book? Why or why not?
5. Use a reading journal to write about your knowledge of this topic. Record what you already know about the topic and what you hope to learn about the topic.
6. Read the book.
7. In your reading journal, record what you learned about the topic and your response to the book.
8. After reading the book complete the activities below.

Content Area Vocabulary
Read the list. What do these words mean?

aspiring
economy
fort
groves
peninsula
pioneers
origin
symbol
theory
tourists
wetlands

After Reading:

Comprehension and Extension Activity

After reading the book, work on the following questions with your child or students in order to check their level of reading comprehension and content mastery.

1. What was Orlando like when it was first founded? (Summarize)
2. Why is Orlando such a popular place for tourism? (Infer)
3. What factors led to Orlando's growth? (Asking questions)
4. What landmarks or attractions would you most like to visit in the city? (Text to self connection)
5. How does the weather in Orlando affect tourism? (Asking questions)

Extension Activity
Create a travel brochure about Orlando. Include several places visitors should see. Write short, exciting paragraphs that highlight the most interesting things about the city. And don't forget to add pictures! You can draw them or print them out from the Internet.

Table of Contents

Orlando Facts

Founded: 1875
Land area: 102.40 square miles
(164.80 square kilometers)
Elevation: 89 feet (27.1 meters) above
sea level
Previous names: Jernigan
Population: 262,372

Average Daytime Temperatures:
winter: 60.2 degrees Fahrenheit
(15.7 degrees Celsius)
spring: 70 degrees Fahrenheit
(21 degrees Celsius)
summer: 92 degrees Fahrenheit
(33.3 degrees Celsius)
fall: 75 degrees Fahrenheit
(44 degrees Celsius)

Ethnic diversity:
White 57.6%
African-American 28.1%
Hispanic or Latino 25.4%
Asian 3.8%
American Indian or Alaska Native .4%
Native Hawaiian or Pacific Islander .1%

City Nicknames:
The City Beautiful
"O" Town

Number of Visitors Annually: 60 million

United States

AL GA

Orlando

Orlando

Florida

City of Lakes

Orlando is located in the center of Florida, a **peninsula** that has such warm weather it is called the "Sunshine State."

The city has more than 100 lakes. Lake Eola is right in the middle of Orlando. It is 80 feet (24.4 meters) deep. A fountain in the center of Lake Eola is the **symbol** for the city.

The Eola Sunday Market, located around the lake, is considered one of the best in Central Florida.

The **origin** of Orlando's name is still a mystery, because there is no official documentation about it. Some think the name comes from a soldier named Orlando Reeves who fought in the Seminole Wars in the 1800s. Could be, but this **theory** is considered local legend by historians.

Orlando Notes
Before it became a busy city, Orlando's land was mostly used for cattle ranching.

Orlando's Lake Lucerne is surrounded by skyscrapers, hotels, and businesses.

Local Landmarks

Orlando is the 77th largest city in the United States. This bustling city was once covered in orange groves and fields for cattle. Now it's filled with tall buildings, such as the Orange County Courthouse, a busy place for lawyers, judges, and citizens.

The Orange County Courthouse complex opened in 1997. It is 416 feet (127 meters) tall and has 1.5 million square feet (139,354 square meters) of floor area.

The Historical Society's mission is to honor the past, explore the present, and shape the future.

The Old Orange County Courthouse is on Central Boulevard. It is now the home of the Historical Society of Central Florida. When it was built in 1927 it cost a million dollars. That would be about 13 million dollars at current values. The new one cost 183 million dollars to build.

There are ghost stories surrounding this old building. Some people say two ghosts live inside the courthouse, a young boy who died nearby and a prisoner who passed away inside his jail cell.

The Old Orlando Railroad Depot was built by Henry Plant, a railroad developer. The train station was dedicated in 1890.

Now better known as Church Street Station, the historic train depot is part of an entertainment complex that features plenty of restaurants and shops. These days, you can still hop on a SunRail train from there to travel throughout Orlando.

The railroad station is one of the area's best examples of Mission Revival style architecture.

Henry Plant
(1819–1899)

The Well's Built Museum of African-American History on West South Street is the largest museum in Central Florida dedicated to African-American history. Dr. William Monroe Wells (1889–1957), an African-American physician, constructed the building in 1926 as a hotel for African-Americans who visited the area.

The museum features authentic 1930s furnishings, as well as artifacts that include official hotel documents and slave records.

Ella Fitzgerald
(1917–1996)

Jackie Robinson
(1919–1972)

Louis Armstrong
(1901–1971)

The South Street Casino, adjacent to the museum, attracted many famous entertainers.

Many famous African Americans used to visit the hotel, including Louis Armstrong and Ella Fitzgerald. Back then, you might have also run into baseball player Jackie Robinson!

11

The historic Greenwood Cemetery was established in 1880 as Orlando's first cemetery. Before it was founded, the people of Orlando had no permanent burial grounds. This led to confusion and lost graves.

A newspaper publisher and politician, Mahlon Gore (1837–1916), campaigned in his paper to establish an official cemetery. Eight Orlando residents put their money together to buy the land. More than 60,000 people are buried there now.

Then and Now

Orlando's history stretches back to the 1500s. Back then, American Indian tribes lived in the area. European settlers arrived in 1536 and started setting up small colonies on the land surrounding Orlando.

You can still see one of the original forts established in 1838. **Fort** Gatlin, built along Lake Gatlin, was used by the 4th United States Artillery during the Second Seminole War.

Fort Gatlin is marked by this stone provided by the Daughters of the American Revolution.

Orlando Notes

Joseph Bumby (1843–1911) was one of Orlando's original **pioneers**. He built a store called Bumby's Hardware Store. Now it's a hamburger restaurant.

Orlando experienced a population boom after World War II ended in 1945. Soldiers returning from war settled down in the area to raise families. Many of them worked at the U.S. Army air bases in Orlando.

Theme park construction in the late 1960s brought even more families to the area. Plenty of jobs became available as hotels, resorts, shopping centers, restaurants, and banks opened up to support the growth. The **economy** boomed. It was a big change from the days when Orlando was mostly full of cows and orange **groves**.

Joe Fowler, Disney vice president of engineering and construction, watches as the land is prepared for the Disney World project in 1969.

Orlando Notes

Colonial Drive was the first highway in Central Florida. It was paved with bricks.

Attractions Aplenty

Construction on the Walt Disney World Resort began in 1967. Now it boasts some of the world's most popular theme parks. The entire resort area is 40 square miles (103.6 kilometers), which is big enough to hold two of New York's Manhattans. That's a lot of play space!

Every day visitors can enjoy a parade on Disney's Main Street in the Magic Kingdom.

Orlando Notes

Cinderella's Castle at the Magic Kingdom was inspired by a castle called Neuschwanstein (noo-shwen-stine) in Germany.

Disney World Park Opening Dates

- Magic Kingdom 1971
- Hollywood Studios 1989
- Epcot 1982
- Animal Kingdom 1998

Orlando is a busy place because of tourism. A lot of people travel to Orlando with their families for vacations. In fact, Orlando can claim more theme parks and entertainment venues than any other place in the world! More than 60 million **tourists** visit Orlando each year for its theme parks. There are more than 140,000 hotel rooms in the city.

Orlando is home to the world's first water park. Wet N' Wild opened in 1977.

Universal Studios Orlando opened in 1990. Islands of Adventure opened next door in 1999. These connected theme parks now get more than 30 million visitors a year.

THE AVERAGE TRAVELER WOULD HAVE TO SPEND 67 DAYS IN ORLANDO TO EXPERIENCE EVERYTHING THERE IS TO DO IN THE CITY.

Visitors are greeted by this large globe when they enter the theme park at Universal Studios.

Animals Everywhere

At SeaWorld Orlando, dolphins, sea lions, and whales perform in shows. Visitors to Discovery Cove can swim with dolphins, stingrays, and other sea creatures.

The Orlando **Wetlands** Park is home to more than 30 species of wildlife, many listed on America's threatened and endangered species list.

Some Orlando attractions offer an up-close experience that makes it all the more fun!

An alligator handler shows just how large these creatures can become while holding the alligator's mouth shut to prevent a bite.

Florida is known for its alligators, and Orlando has a place you can see them up close–safely! Gatorland opened in 1949. The 110-acre (44.5 hectare) theme park and wildlife preserve has thousands of alligators and crocodiles. You can even zipline above the animals.

Alligators are considered living dinosaurs. They've been around for millions of years. But they're not the only dinosaurs in town. The Orlando Science Center has a life-size Tyrannosaurus Rex skeleton. The center has four floors of interactive exhibits, including a planetarium theater for stargazing.

City of Stars

Aspiring actors, dancers, and musicians often move to Orlando to start their careers. The city is known for entertainment. There are all kinds of shows, from concerts to comedies, to mysteries and circus performances. And what does every good show need? Great performers, of course!

Actors are hired by Orlando theme parks to interact with guests.

Some well-known celebrities started their acting and music careers in Orlando. *The Mickey Mouse Club* was a variety show combining songs and skits that entertained audiences from 1955 to 1996. Britney Spears, Justin Timberlake, Christina Aguilera, and Ryan Gosling all got their start on the Mickey Mouse Club.

The Mickey Mouse Club cast gathers for a photo in 1956.

Britney Spears   Justin Timberlake   Christina Aguilera   Ryan Gosling

The Orlando Film Commission encourages filmmakers to move to the area to take advantage of the region's state-of-the-art soundstages and interesting locations. The area is one of the busiest film, TV show, and commercial production centers in the United States.

While visiting Orlando, it isn't unusual to see a film crew shooting a scene for an upcoming movie.

Orlando Notes

The films Tomorrowland, Apollo 13, and Days of Thunder were filmed in Orlando.

23

Notable Orlandoans

The first person to cross the Atlantic Ocean in a gas balloon was Joseph Kittinger. He made the historic flight in 1978. Joseph grew up in Orlando and later joined the U.S. Air Force. He is also famous for setting the world record for the longest skydive from a height greater than 19 miles (30.6 kilometers).

Captain John Watts Young is an astronaut from Orlando. He was the ninth person to walk on the moon and the commander of the Apollo 16 mission.

Joseph Kittinger dives from a balloon with an unbelievable view below.

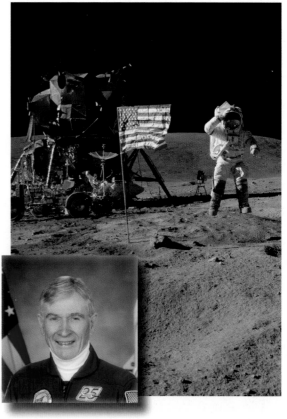

John Watts Young takes a jump from the surface of the moon while saluting the American flag.

Jack Kerouac
(1922–1969)

More than 50 writers from the U.S. and other countries have lived at the Kerouac house since 2000.

Jack Kerouac lived in Orlando in 1957-58, about the same time his classic book *On the Road* was published. He is known for pioneering the Beat Generation, a group of authors whose literature explored and influenced American culture after World War II.

Jack's restored home now serves as a writing retreat for authors. The Kerouac Project allows writers to live in the home rent-free so they can focus on writing their books.

Orlando Sports

Shaquille O'Neal started his legendary National Basketball Association career in Orlando. The seven foot, one inch (215.9 centimeter) tall superstar was draft by the NBA's Orlando Magic in 1992. He led the team to the NBA finals in 1995.

Shaquille O'Neal

Want to catch a game? You won't see Shaquille–he's retired now–but you can see the other Magic stars on the court at the Amway Center in Downtown Orlando.

The Amway Center can hold over 20,000 people, which makes this venue the perfect place to watch a game!

Shaquille O'Neal is one of the most popular players in NBA history.

The Orlando Magic isn't the only team that calls the Amway Center home. The Orlando Predators arena football team and the Orlando Solar Bears hockey team also play there.

The modern design of the Amway Center appeals to more than sports fans. The Center is also used for concerts and other entertainment events.

The Orlando Citrus Bowl opened in 1936. It was originally built as a Works Progress Administration project by President Franklin D. Roosevelt (1882–1945). Since then, it has been expanded and renovated. The 65,000 seat stadium hosts college football games, National Football League pre-season games, and concerts.

Orlando City Lions Kevin Molina leaps over Rochester Rhinos Kevin Duckett at the Citrus Bowl.

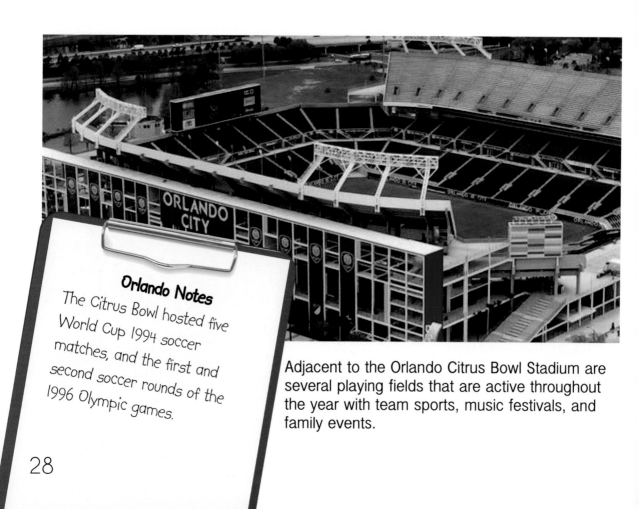

Orlando Notes
The Citrus Bowl hosted five World Cup 1994 soccer matches, and the first and second soccer rounds of the 1996 Olympic games.

Adjacent to the Orlando Citrus Bowl Stadium are several playing fields that are active throughout the year with team sports, music festivals, and family events.

Timeline

1875
Town of Jernigan is incorporated; it's later renamed Orlando.

1889
The Old Orlando Railroad Depot (Church Street Station) is built.

1905
Orlando City Hall is built.

1927
The Orange County Courthouse is built.

1940
The Orlando Army Air Base is established.

1957
Orange County Historical Commission established.

1971
Disney World's Magic Kingdom opens for business.

1976
Orlando International Airport opens.

1984
Orlando Science Center opens.

1990
Universal Orlando theme park opens.

2012
ECHL's Orlando Solar Bears team is founded.

1880
South Florida Railroad begins operating.

1892
Lake Eola Park is established.

1926
The Well's Built Hotel opens for business.

1928
The Orlando Municipal Airport opens.

1949
Gatorland opens.

1960
Central Florida Museum opens.

1973
Sentinel Star newspaper begins publication; SeaWorld Orlando theme park opens.

1983
Orange County Convention Center opens.

1989
Orlando Arena (now the Amway Arena) opens; NBA's Orlando Magic team is founded.

1991
Orlando Predators arena football team forms.

Glossary

aspiring (uh-SPIRE-ing): trying to become something

economy (i-kah-nuh-mee): the system of buying, selling, making things and managing money in a place

fort (fort): a structure that is built to survive enemy attacks

groves (groves): groups of trees growing or planted near one another, as in an orange grove

peninsula (puh-nin-suh-luh): a piece of land that sticks out from a larger landmass and is almost completely surrounded by water

pioneers (pye-un-NEERS): people who explore unknown territory and settle there

origin (or-i-jin): the point where something starts, or the cause of something

symbol (sim-buhl): a design or an object that stands for, suggests, or represents something else

theory (THEER-ee): an idea based on some facts or evidence but not proven

tourists (TOOR-ists): people who travel and visit a place for pleasure

wetlands (wet-landz): lands where there is an abundance of moisture in the soil

Index

Show What You Know

1. What lake is located at the center of Orlando?
2. How have theme parks changed Orlando since its early days?
3. Name two historic buildings or sites in Orlando.
4. What was special about the Well's Built Hotel?
5. Where can you find an original fort from the 1800s?

Websites to Visit

www.visitorlando.com

www.cityoforlando.net

www.osc.org

About the Author

Melanie Waxler is a former television news reporter now working in media relations. When she is not working, you will often find her writing stories, something she's done since she was a child. Melanie shares a love of reading and writing with her two young sons and her journalist husband.

Meet The Author!
www.meetREMauthors.com

www.rourkeeducationalmedia.com

PHOTO CREDITS: Cover: © jodi jacobson; macsim; Susan Chiang; Title Page: © Lorraine Boogich; Page 4, 29: © Evelyn M. Peyton; Page 5, 29: © Richard J Gaydos; Page 6: © Rabbit75; Page 7: © Carl Stewart; Page 8, 9, 13, 24, 25: © Wikipedia; Page 9: © NE2; Page 10: © Ebyabe; Page 11: © William P Gottlieb, Library of Congress, Cowles Communications Inc., Page 12: © Bruce Dowlen; Page 13: © John Stanton; Page 15: © Jim Kerlin/AP Images; Page 16: © Andres Balcazar; Page 17, 29: © Asterixvs; Page 18, 29: © Kamira; Page 19: © targovcom; Page 20, 29: © Kphotos6411; Page 21: © Libo Tang; Page 22: © Macfadden Publications, Frazer Harrison, Steven Lovekin, Jason Merritt, Vito Amati; Page 24: © USAF, NASA; Page 26: © Aguina, Wickedgood; Page 27: © Jason Doly; Page 28: © Cal Sport Media/Alamy Stock Photos, Kitch; Page 29: © Mattkaiser77

Edited by: Keli Sipperley

Illustrations by: Caroline Romanet

Cover and interior design by: Jen Thomas

Library of Congress PCN Data

Dropping in on Orlando / Melanie Waxler
 ISBN 978-1-68191-402-2 (hard cover)
 ISBN 978-1-68191-444-2 (soft cover)
 ISBN 978-1-68191-482-4 (e-Book)
Library of Congress Control Number: 2015951568

Printed in the United States of America, North Mankato, Minnesota

Also Available as:

ROURKE'S
e-Books